To Melda & Brian

Best Wishes

from

Leo

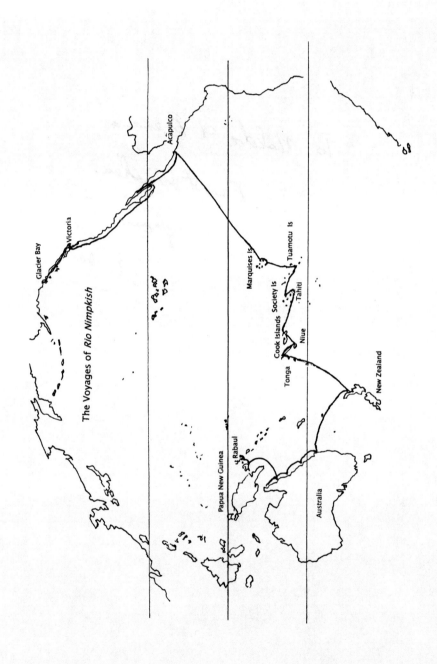

The Voyages of *Rio Nimpkish*

Red Tomatoes

Les MacNeill

*We at Trafford believe that it is the responsibility of us all, as both individuals
and corporations, to make choices that are environmentally and socially sound.
You, in turn, are supporting this responsible conduct each time you purchase a
Trafford book, or make use of our publishing services. To find out how you are
helping, please visit www.trafford.com/responsiblepublishing.html*

*Our mission is to efficiently provide the world's finest, most comprehensive
book publishing service, enabling every author to experience success.
To find out how to publish your book, your way, and have it available
worldwide, visit us online at www.trafford.com/10510*

www.trafford.com

North America & international
toll-free: 1 888 232 4444 (USA & Canada)
phone: 250 383 6864 ♦ fax: 250 383 6804
email: info@trafford.com

The United Kingdom & Europe
phone: +44 (0)1865 722 113 ♦ local rate: 0845 230 9601
facsimile: +44 (0)1865 722 868 ♦ email: info.uk@trafford.com

10 9 8 7 6 5 4 3

Dedication

To a very special person:

She stood by me in the early days
when the doctors didn't think I would survive.

As well, her head injury was a concussion,
giving her serious headaches
and other problems.

In spite of all that,
she always kept in touch
with so much work that we required,
an offshore trip,
everything else that had to be set up and organized.

When my life carried on
and my several years of rehabilitation continued,
she was still there to stand by me.

I could not have done it without her.

I hope the love that has kept us alive
will continue as long as we can continue.

Love to Marcia.

Acknowledgement

I want to thank all of our family,
friends, and acquaintances
who helped us so much through this difficult period.

I don't want to list names for fear of leaving anyone out.

You all did so much for us
and it meant everything to have you there
and to know how you care.

Thanks.

Table of Contents

Prologue

EVERYTHING IS SO GREY. I don't know what is happening. I can see but only a bit. Now it's grey again. Like a dream, it comes and goes. I open my eyes again but nothing is really real. I glimpse things that I don't understand. Sometimes it seems like something I know but it disappears; then it comes back again. This time I know that I open my eyes. It is very grey. Or is it? Now it's gone again, it's spinning about but going nowhere, in circles like in water. I see it again and then I pass out.

I don't know how long I was in a coma before I wake up. It is brighter now. I don't know what is happening but I am awake again. This time people are talking to me. I don't know them but they ask me questions. There is pain; my body hurts all over and I am not able to stop it. All I want to do is move to a different, more comfortable position but someone keeps telling me not to move. Why can't I move? What has happened to me? Why won't someone tell me what is happening? I go back to sleep and hours later I wake up to try again for movement, to get up, to get away, anything. I feel anger building up in me and I try to talk. I want to speak to someone, to tell them who I am, to ask them what is happening. All I get are funny sounds from my voice. I try again but nothing comes out. There are no words, just strange sounds coming out of my mouth. What has happened to me? Dear Lord, what has happened to me? I fight as hard as I can but my arms are being held tight, and my body is being held tight. I will fight my way out. I don't know how but I will. But it hurts and then I fall asleep. When I wake again my arms are still tied but I feel much brighter. I seem to have a few glimpses of the past, or do I? Where am I? How did I get here?

Chapter 1

Leaving Victoria

I THINK EVERYONE IN THE world at some time dreams of being a sailor. I was no different and perhaps I started sooner than most. When I was 6 or 7 I lived in Halifax with my family of three sisters and four brothers. We were given a lot of freedom, which no doubt started my adventuresome spirit at a young age. As it was, I had my first sight of the sea at the local small boat dock that we called the Dingle. I was by myself and the ocean seemed enormous. It was the first time that I had seen anything that big. I found a nearby dinghy that I "borrowed" to try rowing which I found to be quite easy. What took work was to return the "borrowed" dinghy quietly back to its owner. The owners didn't mind as long as the dinghy was returned and tied up properly. This was the beginning of my love for the ocean and my dreams of sailing. I am sure that the borrowed dinghy is long gone but I have carried on and have added years to my age. One thing that has not changed is my love of the sea and of boats.

From the East Coast I moved to Victoria where I worked as a respiratory therapist. I enjoyed this interesting, challenging work but whenever vacation time came I went sailing. I planned sailing trips that grew longer and longer and that became more and more interesting. As my eyes opened to the world, the world opened up to me. While the world itself didn't become any larger, with each exploration it became larger and more beautiful in my eyes. After a day of sailing I would anchor my boat, look at the sky, enjoy the beauty all around me and think: I still have another day tomorrow to enjoy this.

Well, the days did go on and most were great. Unfortunately, time never allows enough days to do everything that we want to do. I became quite familiar with a few places where I sailed often, and I explored other areas that I didn't come to know as well. In 1986 I circumnavigated Vancouver Island stopping at Haida Gwai. I fell in love with the area and made another trip there a few years later.

I was living my dream of sailing but I was dreaming about sailing while thinking of work. There was too much conflict between the two of them so in 1995 I took early retirement, allowing me to become a full time sailor. Life became much busier as I worked on my third and latest boat, the *Rio Nimpkish* (meaning Big Fish). It was a 39-foot Corbin, an extremely well-built boat which I bought because it was designed for open ocean sailing. As usual, the interior was not laid out the way I wanted. Fortunately, I was very handy with tools and liked woodworking so making changes while travelling became a natural part of sailing. I had plans for an open-ended trip south to Mexico, then west through the South Pacific, possibly on through Asia to Europe.

At that time I met my partner, Marcia, who was an avid runner and traveller. She was changing jobs and as we got along well together I suggested that she join me in a short "shake down" trip to Alaska prior to my trip south and beyond. This preparatory trip would not only help me to get my boat in great shape for the big trip, but would also take me to an exciting area full of charm and Russian history that I wanted to see. As well, it would be an opportunity to see and hear the magnificent Alaskan glaciers.

With great expectation I began another adventure. I loaded

up the necessary charts, the tools that I might need, and of course lots of music. One of my good sailing friends planned to join me in his boat. I said goodbye to Marcia who continued to work, and sailed north toward Alaska. There were so many beautiful places to see along the way that I didn't have much time to visit, but I did stop in Prince Rupert where Marcia flew to join me.

Many passages that we travelled were narrow, twisted channels not suitable for sailing, so we spent much of our time motoring, which I didn't enjoy. However, the endless scenery kept opening up like a photograph: every corner we turned presented a new panorama, each one more beautiful than the last. How could anyone look at such beauty without wanting to be a part of this awesome vista? Yet this vision turned my eye inward, to store the beauty within my head. I always admire those with the gift of making beautiful pictures such as a professional photographer or a talented painter. But perhaps someone like me gets the best of all for I can keep the scene in my mind to remember for perpetuity.

There is a great deal of sea traffic in this area so I had to be careful not only of fishing boats but also cruise ships, which increased in number as we travelled north. Although the days were still bright until late in the evening I could feel them shortening. As I knew that before long the weather would change and winter would be upon us, I took advantage of the long days for travelling, but we were reaching the end of our journey. We planned to finish and turn south at Glacier Bay as we had heard so much about it, and wanted to experience seeing and hearing the action of the glaciers at close range. Entrance to Glacier Bay Park is limited and reservations are usually needed, so we booked and waited outside the Park at Gustavus for several days for a permit to enter. Eventually our turn came and we finally sailed into Glacier Bay.

The scenery was everything we had expected but we had

one setback. While leaving a small quiet cove, Blue Mouse Cove, I hit some rocks. As I thought the tide was low and rising I immediately stopped, waiting to float off. I was wrong, as the tide was high and falling so this was, of course, the worst thing that I could do at this time of extreme neap tides. As I tried turning *Rio Nimpkish* with no success it became obvious that I was stuck. With water around the boat dropping fast I went to work as quickly as I could, using logs to support the hull as the boat began to lean over. In the end no harm was done to the boat as the cove was very calm, just a definite bit of embarrassment done to me; especially when I see pictures of *Rio Nimpkish* on its side with water trickling by and no place to go. We spent the whole day waiting for the tide to change instead of being near the glaciers as we had planned. Well now we sure knew where Blue Mouse Cove was.

From that disastrous day we moved to Reid Inlet and could not have found a more picturesque spot. We anchored a safe distance from the main glacier but were still able to hear the rumbling and groaning that carried on all night long. The next morning, while having breakfast in our cockpit, we were immediately given a display of huge hunks of ice calving away from the glacier, then dispersing into smaller "bergy bits". It was an amazing sight that we will never forget. We planned to row ashore for a hike but as we were choosing an area, we noticed that it was already occupied by a big grizzly bear. Deciding to leave the area to him we gave up our idea of a hike for that day and left for John Hopkins Glacier, the upper limit of boat travel in the Bay. The next day we returned to Gustavus in time for Marcia to fly back for work. Time goes so fast! We arrived on time and I found out later that Marcia had arrived safely in Victoria.

I was on my way again, alone, a little bit sad, but searching for new adventure. I made several stops on the way south taking in Petersburg with its interesting Russian history, and the Indian stockade in Sitka National Park, where the Tlingit tribe made a last stand against Russian settlers. I spent time in the exciting old town of Sitka, but felt the days shorten even more. Although the weather was still pleasant and warm I felt pressured to head home at a safe pace before the season and the weather changed. As much as it bothered me to pass by so many beautiful spots I returned relatively quickly, taking advantage of fortunate weather to arrive back home with no further mishaps along the way.

Marcia was in Victoria finishing up work and upon my return we started preparing for our Mexico trip. We spent the next year preparing, and in September 1996, with all the usual fanfare of parties, pictures and farewells, we said our goodbyes to friends and family. We departed from the dock. We were on our way!

Chapter 2

Mexico

IN SEPTEMBER 1996 WE left Victoria for points south and west. As Marcia was not an experienced sailor we made short hops from port to port, south along the West Coast of the United States. The fall weather was mild and the wind was light, so again we motored part of the time to make some stops in the huge inland waterways of Portland and Astoria. We then moved out into the open waters of the Pacific to the west. With good winds behind us and bright sunshine above us, this was what life was all about! These were the sort of days that couldn't get much better.

The weather stayed beautiful past Eureka, giving us nice rough seas to travel in as we passed Cape Mendicino on our way to San Francisco. To me, the sailing was always fun, but Marcia never felt quite that way. But I must say that one of our pictures tells a slightly different story of how she felt one day, for she looks like she wants to be on the wheel for the whole day. We planned to explore the San Francisco Bay area for a few days. As our stay stretched over a month we knew that we had to leave before we spent all of our cruising funds during our first stop. Extending our planned time in an area we loved became the theme of our trip.

Our last US port was San Diego where I made final boat preparations while Marcia stocked the boat. San Diego is typically a last stop for cruisers heading south to prepare and provision and to wait until the official end of hurricane season, as many insurance companies will not cover a boat south of San Diego prior to November 1. We paid close attention to prevailing weather conditions and planned never to be on the boat in a hurricane area during hurricane season.

In December we finally entered Mexican waters and felt that our "real" trip had begun. Our first overnight trip in Mexico was one I will remember for many years, for of all the times we sailed in rough weather, this was the time that affected us the most. Leaving Ensenada we were struck by the tail end of California's famous Santa Ana winds. Fortunately, I realized something was coming so I was able to prepare the sailing gear. Marcia had to be tied in the galley while cooking so that she wouldn't be knocked about inside the boat. I was secure in the cockpit to tend to the lines as required.

The self steering gear worked beautifully. We had no trouble with the boat throughout the night while the wind blew ferociously, all night and into the next morning. Finally we were able to come closer to shore. Some Mexican fishers guided us by radio into some offshore islands where we got some well-needed rest and connected with two other boats that had also weathered the storm. No doubt we have many stories about this trip, and as we tell them they probably get bigger each time. But for sure this is the one that I remember the most.

We visited the usual tourist spots- Mazatlan, Puerto Vallarta, Manzanillo, Zihuatanejo, Acupulco, which allowed family and friends to visit. Getting to know Mexico was so exciting that we spent two years learning a bit of Spanish and trying to understand the culture. Before long, I had to make up my mind: shall I stay in Mexico, or shall I carry on with my real desire, to reach out to the rest of the world which I hadn't seen yet?

Mexico has sites that amaze travellers from around the world, but what I liked most was visiting remote areas, accessible only by boat, to meet the locals and the villagers. At Mulege we met a fellow named 'Shipwreck Lee' who was very interesting. He lost his sailboat in a grounding off South America a few years earlier. He then did a bit of land travel and plunked himself down in Bahia Coyote (Coyote Bay) where he provided a radio net, rides to town plus workshop services and book trades for visiting yachties.

One day I went with Lee to the cockfights, a giant size melee. The cocks represent two districts, both of which had many residents in the audience. The height of the excitement, the competition, as well as too much cerveza, were just the right ingredients for a brawl which went on for a short time until the beer was cut off and the police arrived.

An added bonus for me was a 200 peso ($30) lottery win on a 20 peso ticket. I managed to cut my profit a bit by purchasing two more tickets thinking I was on a roll, which I wasn't, so I quit while I was still ahead. Lee entertained us for the rest of the night with exciting stories of his past. In years to come I hope to have the opportunity to meet him again.

Another highlight was the Barranca del Cobra, Copper Canyon. We left our boat at a marina and set off to Los Mochis for a 7 day trip chock full of adventure. A week only allowed enough time to see a very small portion of the enormous canyon, as it is four times larger than the Grand Canyon.

It was entered by Europeans in 1564, but has only been accessible to tourists since 1961 when the Chihuahua al Pacifico Railway was completed. The railway runs through 5 climate zones from sea level to 2400 metres, features 86 tunnels and 37 bridges. It took 89 years and $US100 million to complete.

The Segunda Class train ride was a real experience in down home Mexican transportation. Everything but chickens came on board as we travelled north into the Sierra Madre mountains in Chihuahua state. At the higher elevations the weather became much cooler, with rain and even hail one day.

The Tarahumara tribe in that area held a special interest for us with their world renowned skill in long distance running. Their name means 'the foot runners' and they have been known to run down deer.

As we travelled from the bottom to the top we could see the switchbacks as we moved along, until finally we reached the breathtaking view. Our trip around the valley was amazing, but it soon ended as we headed home to the boat.

Each year we returned to Victoria either for Christmas or during the June-to-October hurricane season when we stored *Rio Nimpkish* on land for safety. We did not plan to spend so much time in Mexico but we fell in love with the people and the country, and had a hard time leaving.

Chapter 3

Crossing the Equator

FINALLY IN MARCH 1999 we left from Acapulco for the Marquises Islands, the most north-easterly islands of French Polynesia. When we left the weather was fine, the sailing was perfect and I was in my usual fine sense of contentment. But as the journey carried on the wind slowly died off and I realized that we were in the devilish doldrums. I had heard about what they were like, what they could do to you, and now I guessed I would find out for myself.

The days continued on and on and on, with continual poor wind as I became more upset over it all. It bothered me more than it affected Marcia, as she would just read or do some cooking or other work to occupy her time, but for me everything was exacerbating my problems. Every time the boat rolled back and forth, exactly the same way, a thousand times a day, every sound drove me crazy. It was the same sound of the slack sailing gear, over and over. There was just absolutely no wind day after day after day, and we could not make any miles. Occasionally we got a few breaths of wind with which I would work the sails as best as I could to cover a little distance.

Around this time we crossed the Equator, but I was so disgruntled that it was anti-climatic and I was in no mood for a Crossing Party. Surprisingly enough, I still have the certificate Marcia made to cheer me up, as she had crossed the Equator several times, but by land. Maybe someday I'll celebrate the event in style.

One day in frustration, for something to do, I tied myself to the boat for a swim. While checking the condition of the boat I noticed the side was totally covered by miniature barnacles about 2 inches long. I could not understand how they would grow in just the length of time that we had been travelling. As this would prevent our movement through the water it was very disturbing to me but I didn't know what to do about it.

While I was thinking about it things began to happen: the skies began to change and we got a few shifts of wind. Light wind perhaps, but still glorious gifts of wind. It continued on for a couple of days and began to build up until we were really once again sailing. As the boat heeled over properly to one side I could see that the high side was clean and had no barnacles. Where did they go? That whole thing was such a strange affair to me. The wind continued intermittently with occasional squalls but before long we had continuous winds and I felt good, we were sailing again! This 35-day trip was our longest passage but we at last arrived in French Polynesia.

This certificate witnesseth that on this
4th day of April in the year of 1999
one former polliwog, namely

James Leslie McNeill

a.k.a. Kishman

did become a full-fledged shell-back by completing the following tasks:

1. crossing the 0 meridian also known as the Equator at a longitude of 124° 44.533 W at precisely 23:21:28

2. paying tribute to the Gods of the Sea, namely Neptune and Poseidon and such other spirits as reign here, and

3. pledging servitude to the lovely and talented helpmate of the Gods, one Marcia, a godess in her own right of cuisine and other feminine wizardry

Chapter 4

French Polynesia

As we arrived in the Marquesas, we were greeted by views of rugged volcanic mountains on lush tropical islands. Everywhere we hiked there were valleys with rivers or streams to stop to see, or to just meander along. We travelled around Hiva Oa, Ua Pou and Nuku Hiva for three weeks, then headed southwest for the Tuamotus. These low sandy islands, surrounded by coral atolls, look like a typical desert island postcard picture.

We sailed for 5 days, looking forward to a stop at Takaroa. While the snorkeling was not as exciting as in the Sea of Cortez, we had a wonderful time just the same. The best treat was the comfortable anchorage in the lagoon, sheltered by a reef. The wonderful protection was welcome after the rolly anchorages of the Marquises Islands.

We started to feel a little bit like land lubbers again since our passage. Being able to have breakfast whenever we want is a real treat. Marcia didn't know how to cook with a level stove. She made sausages and eggs on our last passage. When she took her eyes off the plate for a moment while serving, the boat lurched and the eggs went flying through the air landing in the sink, followed by some colourful language from her.

We left this lagoon for the next atoll, Toau, 100 knots away. We wanted to stop here because of our interest in pearl farming, the predominant activity in the atoll. While we toured the beautiful atolls, I would have loved to spend more time to see how their aquaculture was set up, but there was just not enough time.

We stopped at Anse Amyot (Amyot Cove) and met Gaston and his family. We spent over two weeks here. On Wednesdays the supply ship from Papeete arrived, so we helped Gaston collect fish from his fish trap and deliver them to the ship. Doing so taught me a lot about catching fish.

We had a full day of spear fishing and looking for coconut crabs. They are a very delicious, large land crab that comes out in the dark.

Not only did we work with the locals during the day, we had dinners with music at night on shore. Word got out about the place; before long a few yachts arrived, then a few more. One night was an exciting one, with lots of music: banjo, guitar, as well as my saxophone. A young local man played spoons, so I loaned him my wooden ones, but he preferred the kitchen variety. He was surprised that I played spoons as well.

Like everything else, there is always so much to do and too little time to do it. Once again we said goodbye, this time to Gaston and Valentine, and traveled on towards Papeete, Tahiti.

After Tahiti, we anchored in beautiful Baie Marie on Mourea for three days. We of course explored the whole island, including Cook's Bay, famous for the Bali Hai Hotel, and Opunohu Bay, famous as well as the backdrop for the movie South Pacific. We went up to nearby Belvedere Lookout and spent time at the ancient marae (temple) where religious rites and sacrifices were carried out in the not so distant past. It gave me a strange feeling to look at it and to walk by it.

After three months touring the beautiful atolls and islands, we left our sailing friends in Bora Bora to carry on alone to our last destination of Maupiti, 28 miles away. The pass into the atoll has a high current running which lessens around noon, but it must be handled with caution, at the right time, as well as in the proper weather. We arrived comfortably although not without apprehension. Once inside, the anchorage was very peaceful and beautiful so in no time we were right at home again.

While we were motoring to the town site a small rowboat had passed by which was out of fuel, so as I was passing them I handed him some gasoline to help him along. He was very happy to get the help and thus was able to motor his way and in return left us with a couple of little fishes which we had for our supper. The day was starting out as a good omen!

The next day Marcia and I went for a run and of course this was quite an occasion for people to talk about, these sailors who go for a run, this is not something they would see happen every day. Some of the kids had a lot of fun with it, though, for I had a few baseball caps that I had saved up for such an occasion. Every time I went ashore I was greeted by cries of 'Chapeau, chapeau' from the kids until I had to respond 'Pas de chapeau.'

In no time at all we knew everybody in the neighbourhood. The kids would swim over to see us for fun and company. One special young fellow who I liked, he was about 12 or 13, would row over to us early in the morning with a fresh brown baguette for Marcia and me, and he wouldn't let me give him any money for it. His name was Fattu, such a terrific kid, as all of them were. We met them all, in ages from about 3 or 4 to 17. One day they took Marcia and I to the watermelon farm. There were more watermelons thrown around and played with that day than were carried home; but I still remember one little girl carrying her little watermelon on her shoulder all the way home by herself. It was quite an exciting day.

Spending so much time with the children and getting to know several of the teenagers left us feeling very vulnerable, as we knew that we would have to depart in the not too distant future. And I think the children were feeling the same way. We had been experiencing a lot of bad weather for a few days, so we spent time with the kids which they enjoyed, playing games and joking around on the boat. We also played music on our tape deck and the girls brought a song to sing and dance to. I thought they looked very good and might possibly have a future as dancers.

They left us for a few hours, then returned with bananas and papayas and asked if we would meet their parents which of course we did. They were just like the children, which of course is just what you would expect so everyone fit in well. After we met all the family, which were many, we made plans for our departure so that we could say goodbye to everyone. The day before we left the neighbours set up a big dinner for everyone in the evening. It was an absolutely wonderful evening; we had so much good food and such a good time. It was certainly one of the highlights of my sailing trips. Four of the teenage girls danced various dances for about two hours which would have made excellent justice to a TV show. Three of their male visiting cousins sang and made music with a banjo, ukulele and guitar. They were equally as good.

Altogether we all had a wonderful and nostalgic evening which we will not forget. We had hoped to get away on time, but unfortunately we had to wait for a whole day to get through the pass, as the sea was so rough that day that it was not passable with the huge breaking seas. We were barely able to leave safely the next day; nevertheless we did manage and then carried on to our next destination of the Cook Islands.

What will lead us there? I know it is always an adventure but at the moment all I can think is that I am quite sad at leaving behind some wonderful friends; my eyes are misted as our boat sails south.

Chapter 5

Cook Islands

OUR LANDFALL WAS AITUTAKI, a small island, where we anchored in the lagoon , and spent a few days. We saw some wonderful contests of singing and dancing in preparation for their Independence Day. A different group danced every night, and they were all spectacular. The best groups go to the capital, Avarua, for the national competition.

We moved on to the main island, Rarotonga. We were not blessed with good weather for the first few weeks, and we had to Med moor, or anchor with the stern tied to the wharf. This is very uncomfortable, as the boat cannot change position with the wind or current.

One thing that made us happy was the delicious ice cream, only fifty cents a cone, so we were there often.

We did hear some of the most beautiful singers that we have ever heard. We were at a church for about half an hour, listening and thinking that we were hearing music on a sound system. When the singing finished, then started again, we realized that it was the congregation, not a choir, singing. It was hard to believe that they could sing in such perfect harmony.

I think Marcia had more fun looking around after church at the hats, so large and brightly adorned, which all of the women wore.

We toured the whole island on a scooter in one day, with

plenty of stops. We also hiked the Cross Island trail, where it was so cold and damp that one friend wore long underwear under her shorts.

Cook Islanders are happy, friendly people, and we enjoyed our time here.

Chapter 6

Niue

WE ARRIVED AT NIUE after a fairly fast trip from Rarotonga. The seas were moderately rough, with 20 to 30 knot winds the whole way. When we arrived we could see the bottom of our anchorage, even to a depth of 90 to 100 feet, due to the very clear water. Niue, one of the world's smallest countries, is really a large block of coral that filters the rain to produce some exceptionally clear water around it. The surrounding sea is protected as well to keep the area clean and the coral undamaged.

In spite of the size of the island, we managed to find much of interest in a short time. How could I not try a smorgasbord featuring flying foxes, so I did. While I would not say they were great, being a bit gritty, at least they were worth a try.

The local market had beautiful furniture made of a local hardwood. They call the seats a love seat for Niueans, or a couch for whites, as the locals are such large people.

Our last night in Niue was rainy, blustery and cool. but it all brightened up with the sound of whales singing, clearly audible through the hull of our boat as we lay in our bunk. This was the first time I have ever heard humpbacks singing, other than on tape, and it was truly fascinating.

Chapter 7

Tonga

WE ARRIVED IN THE Vava'u group, Tonga, and the change to a quiet, well protected anchorage and inland sailing brought nostalgia for the Gulf Islands around Victoria. There are numerous anchorages with reasonable depth, waters that make relaxation easy.

The Tongans are quite friendly but not as relaxed as Mexicans. Here both men and women wear a pareau or wrap around skirt, with a waist sash which, I understand, is meant to show respect.

The big event is that our trip coincided with the day that the King of Tonga arrived for the Dawning of the New Millennium Feast, Sept 25, filmed by New Zealand TV. This island, just west of the International Date Line, is the first to see a new day.

I got my first and best look at the King as he rode through the downtown area with his guards. The next day, Saturday, he spoke at the 100 Days to the New Millennium Celebration that we attended, properly attired and seated on the ground. There was wonderful choir singing and several speeches that we didn't understand as they were in Tongan. However, we did hear the King's voice and even got a few glimpses of his head above the crowd as we took our place.

The afternoon featured a huge outdoor feast for many people, including much dancing and singing. We watched but did not eat although we were told that we could.

After this exciting visit, we explored beautiful diving areas all within close sailing distance. But soon, again, we had to start getting ready for our trip to New Zealand.

Preparing to leave the Tongatapu Group and Tonga had us waiting for a good weather window. The weather stayed miserable for a few days, but finally we were able to make our exit, and in 8 days we arrived in New Zealand.

Chapter 8

New Zealand and Australia

WE THEN TRAVELLED WEST and south stopping in the
Cook Islands and Niue before arriving in Tonga
where again we waited for favourable weather.
Storms arise frequently in this area of the Pacific and the Tonga
to New Zealand trip can be dangerous so we wanted the best
possible conditions. Eventually the weather forecast was good
and we left, arriving in New Zealand in November 1999.

Again, we fell in love with New Zealand and spent eigh-
teen months touring both in our boat and by land, with a few
flights back to Victoria and Australia. These excursions helped
our immigration situation. While it is easy to obtain a boat
permit, as the authorities recognize the dangers of sailing during storm season and readily accept safe sailing plans, visas
for people are another issue. Sometimes leaving and obtaining
a new visa is the only way to meet immigration requirements.
However, we found time for a few visits inland, leaving our
boat in the town basin at Whangerai ("Fungaray"). We missed
being rocked to sleep on board at night, but did not miss the
occasional rude awakening when the wind howled in the rig-
ging to call us topside for our shift at anchor watch.

We began one adventure by bussing to Whitianga on the
eastern shore of the Cormandel Peninsula. As this area is a
mountainous rainforest, we travelled a winding mountain

highway, which occasionally opened up to lush farming valleys, populated with the usual multitude of cattle and sheep. Most of the time, however, we rode through dense woodland, beautiful and green, with many topical ferns and low growing foliage plants mixed in with larger trees.

Unfortunately, the forests suffer from the same thoughtless, destructive clearcutting as do British Columbia forests. However, as a credit to the government, over the past few years large National Reserves were set aside. In them are many wonderful hiking trails, or "tramping tracks" as they are called in Kiwi Land. Here we saw the beauty of first growth forests with magnificent giant Kauri trees. One felled stump in Whitianga was so huge that it became a dance floor for 30 dancing couples! We didn't see anything that immense, but did see a few amazingly large trees.

Before forestry cut itself out of business, this area was very prosperous from shipping Kauris, much sought after for use as ship masts in the early days of sail, throughout the world. This all ended in the early 1900s. The main industry shifted to tourism, and one attraction is the hot water beach. Dig a hole in the sand at low tide and you can sit in it as it fills with hot water runoff from the area's hot springs.

We spent two days hiking to the top of Mount Maunganui, Tauranga, for a wonderful view of the surrounding ocean and city. Next was Rotorua, city of hot springs, natural mud baths, Maori feasts and dances, multitudes of coffee shops, and a host of daredevil entertainment for the young and foolish: jet boat rides up canyons, sky diving, and of course bungy jumping. You can't miss the town as you approach for the smell of sulphur in the air. However, it's not an obnoxious smell and you get used to it before the end of your visit.

We enjoyed walks to the boiling craters, geysers and bubbling hot mud pools. On par with this was an ancestral style Maori feast with native dancing. Men dominate the Haka dance. While women play a role, they are very much over-shadowed by the men attempting to determine whether a visitor is friend or foe by trying to scare them off. I think seeing the Haka almost justifies the airfare here.

At Taupo we definitely felt the effect of travelling south with several nights of frost and, one day, snow. This area is also full of hot springs. Returning from one hike, we followed a hot stream to a delightful pool of beautiful, clear, clean hot water where we soaked our tired muscles for some time before resuming our journey. The only thing missing was a bottle of wine.

Here we travelled east to Napier. In 1933 it suffered a 7.9 magnitude earthquake, which caused major destruction and large loss of life. The city was rebuilt in the art deco style of the time, and is now famous for art deco architecture and festivals. On the eve of our departure, the city hosted an impressive beach party with entertainment followed by a huge beach fire and dance. Marcia was impressed as she thought it was our farewell party. I had to disappoint her by telling her that it was a celebration of winter solstice.

We headed north to warmer weather and home. We were happy to be back on board *Rio Nimpkish*, but were not too excited to find that a pair of large herons had taken up residence on the bow, leaving loads of organic calling cards all over the deck.

We left New Zealand in June 2001 intending to sail north and west to Brisbane, Australia. This was another challenging passage, due not to length but to weather. Front after front moved over us, their winds making a direct route impossible. We could sail west or north but not north-west. We were ready to give up and sail north to New Caledonia, then Southwest to Australia when the weather changed and we enjoyed some great sailing, however a trip that should have taken a week took 12 days.

Brisbane was chosen as our destination so that we could

compete in the WAVA Games, the World Veterans' Athletic Championships in July 2001. We both ran several races and had a wonderful time. Running has always been a passion for both of us.

We had been sailing for 5 years so we now began to discuss options for returning to Victoria. The usual choices are: 1) through the Red Sea and Suez Canal to Europe; or 2) around the Cape of Good Hope, South Africa to South America. Both of these choices require a trip through the Panama Canal before a sail north to Victoria. After considering all of the routes, the potential weather conditions and current political situations, we decided to make a Pacific Ocean circumnavigation; to sail north through the western pacific to Japan and the Aleutian Islands, then to Alaska and south to Victoria. Mindful of political unrest in the area we chose our route carefully, hoping to avoid trouble. We were encouraged after meeting a couple whom had sailed our planned route and had such a wonderful time they planned to do it again. This plan took us to Cairns, the last port of exit on Australia's East Coast where we eagerly prepared to leave for Papua New Guinea on another new adventure, one which I didn't expect.

Chapter 9

Papua New Guinea

WHILE WE PREPARED TO leave Australia the September 11 attack on the World Trade Center occurred. This confirmed our decision to avoid the Red Sea and reinforced our decision to return home to be with family and friends. Just as we were ready to depart I flew to Vancouver for a family funeral. While Marcia waited she filled the boat with provisions, small gifts and children's clothing for the locals we hoped to meet en route, so that once I returned we could leave.

I had a challenge explaining myself to Australian Immigration in the post 9-11 climate as a single man flying with little luggage planning to stay in the country for only one day. However, I managed, and immediately processed the boat to leave Australia the next day for Papua New Guinea (PNG). We sailed north and east through many beautiful sparsely inhabited small islands arriving in Rabaul, New Britain in early December. By mid December we were ready to sail to Kavieng on New Ireland to spend Christmas and New Year with friends. However, the alternator was not working. It had been 'fixed' once but the repair only lasted a few minutes so we were trying a different repair shop impatiently waiting to get underway again.

On December 11 we went ashore in the morning to hike

up a hill overlooking the harbour as the view was reputed to
be excellent. I decided to have a slow leisurely run of about 45
minutes just to keep in shape before we set sail again. Before
returning to the boat I hoped to pick up the alternator to in-
stall so that we would be ready to leave the next day. I was already feeling excited again, anticipating getting on our way to
Japan, the Aleutians and Canada, looking forward to the thrill
of single-handing the controls of *Rio Nimpkish* with Marcia taking care of the interior. How do you go from being a talented
sailor to being left for dead or mortally injured in a split second? From this moment on my life was no longer the same!

We walked along the airport road on our way to see the
view from the former governor's mansion. We were unsure
which path to take as the volcano eruption in 1994 ruined the
roads, now only accessible by 4-wheel drive vehicle or on foot.
We met a young man who showed us the way. He wore only
shorts; no shoes or shirt as is common in PNG. He carried
a stick resembling a field hockey stick so Marcia asked if he
played hockey, and he said yes. He certainly looked young
and fit enough to be a professional athlete. He was friendly
and chatted with us as we walked up the hill. On the way he
showed us the War Memorial to those who lost their lives in
WWII and showed us a shortcut up the hill. We continued up
to the old mansion, an interesting looking ruin with a spectacular view. However, people were living in the building so
we didn't feel that it was appropriate to go inside so, disap-
pointed, we headed down the hill.

I have no recollection of most of this walk nor of the stranger
who accompanied us. Marcia told me that we stopped for a
snack at an uninhabited ruin of a house in a small clearing,
making our usual jokes about a coat of paint and curtains
turning it into home. We sat for awhile, then she said "I guess
its time to head down" and looked towards me.

The stranger was behind me, his stick raised in the air; just then she saw him bring it down hard on my head. She had no time to shout a warning to me. Many thoughts instantaneously rushed into her mind: if only she had looked up sooner and had had time to warn me I might have reacted and avoided a direct blow to my head; if I had moved just a little the blow might have glanced off or hit me somewhere else. She knew that I was unconscious from the moment I was struck as I immediately fell to the ground, limp and soundless. Why did the stranger do that, she thought? She was so shocked but she thought run, run as fast as you can. Then no, the stranger might follow and hit her; she would not be near Les and someone might find one but not both of us, better stay together. Her next thought was scream, make as much noise as possible, someone might hear or maybe it will scare him off.

She has no recollection of the stranger approaching her as the next thing she recalls is standing, looking at me still lying on the ground, with several women standing around us. It was several hours later and getting dark. She knew that we had to get off the mountain soon or we would be unable to find the way and would have to spend the night there. She also knew that I needed medical attention, but of course had no idea of the extent of my injuries. She kicked me, saying "Come on Les, get up, we have to get down before dark". A lady took her hand and gently said "He can't walk. We will have to carry him. The men have gone for a door". A door? Why on earth do we need a door? She was not in pain and had no memory of being beaten as well, although there was blood all over her shirt. She had a vague idea that she must have fallen and maybe suffered a nosebleed.

The lady holding her hand asked if she could walk. Marcia said yes just as several men arrived with a door that became a makeshift stretcher for me. As we started down the hill she thought about how long it would take. She was sure we couldn't get down before dark, but the men took a path pretty much straight down the hill. They continually changed positions as we descended, holding the door over their heads in a masterful job of keeping the door level and of keeping me on it. The lady holding her hand encouraged her all the way down. She says that she felt that we were in safe hands, being cared for, and she knew that the locals were in control and were taking us to medical help. As we reached the bottom of the hill, two or three miles from the hospital, and started walking toward the town, a pickup truck appeared and loaded me, Marcia, and all the locals in the back and took off for the hospital.

Once we arrived Marcia talked to a doctor who asked if we had children. She thought he meant on the boat, children needing care, so she said no. He asked if she wanted to call anyone and she thought, "If I telephone to say Les was beaten up and if anyone asks how bad is he, I don't know yet, so I'll wait until I know Les' prognosis".

I didn't seem to have any broken bones but was deeply unconscious, neither moving nor making any sound. She still had no idea that she had been beaten, as she felt all right and no one seemed concerned with the way she looked.

The doctor talked with her for a few minutes then said, "We are going to take you upstairs to clean you up". Marcia expected to be treated by a nurse for minor abrasions with alcohol swabs and ointment, then sent home while I was admitted. The next thing she knew it was late the next day.

Chapter 10

Rabaul to Australia

I HAVE NO RECOLLECTION OF our time in the Rabaul hospital as I was in a coma. Marcia says that our time there is fuzzy to her as well. She awoke in bed in a large ward with me in the adjacent bed. She had an intravenous tube in her arm but never asked what was being administered. I was in the next bed with my head bandaged and an IV tube in my arm. Apparently I was moving my arms and legs and muttering. Marcia thought: Good, no casts so no broken bones and he can talk (although my mumbling was gibberish) and he can walk (so she assumed as my limbs moved). What more do we need? Little did she know that I had suffered major skull fractures, eight in all, and a serious brain injury. Over the next few days I periodically became active, thrashing and trying to tear off the bandages. An older patient in our ward had several grandsons visiting him almost constantly who immediately would come to hold me still and to send for a nurse. She would adjust the IV and soon I would be still again, no doubt in a drug-induced sleep.

People we knew and other expatriates heard about our situation, knew we needed to be medically evacuated, and started collecting funds. They visited, bringing food and asking what they could do for us. Marcia remembers telling two men from the yacht club how to get into the locked boat, where our passports and other documents were, and that we had medical coverage with "a big company" as she couldn't remember the name Blue Cross. They contacted the local immigration office to find out our last names. One friend brought soup that his wife had made and asked if Marcia had seen herself yet. She responded that there were no mirrors in the hospital to which he replied, "Good. Don't look".

News of our attack spread quickly and was broadcast by Canadian news agencies. Unfortunately, this was how our families and friends were informed. Marcia planned to telephone as soon as she knew the extent of our injuries but she was unconscious after our initial hospitalization for about 24 hours, and by then the news was out. The local expats developed the film in our cameras thinking we might have a photo of our attacker. Then, learning that we had medical insurance, they used the funds collected as a reward for information about our attacker. He was apprehended quickly in his own village. One of the expatriates told Marcia "Don't worry, we got the guy who did it and he is in jail. If he escapes someone will kill him as he has brought dishonour to his community". She was not sure that she wanted to hear that last bit of information. However, he remained in jail and by March 2002 was sentenced to 20 years hard labour for the attack. The remaining funds were later used to look after our boat.

By this time friends and family in Victoria were organizing our medical evacuation and Marcia was receiving telephone calls from Canada. This was an interesting experience as hospital telephone service terminated every 5 minutes to prevent people from running up huge bills. However, by the time she shuffled with her IV pole to the office much of the five minutes would be over. She knew that medical evacuation was planned, as there is no neurosurgeon in PNG. She spoke several times with a Blue Cross representative who, in the first call, estimated the cost of my treatment less the amount of medical coverage that we had, and asked how Marcia expected to pay for the balance. As a Canadian, Marcia was fairly shocked by this abrupt request for payment up front. In subsequent calls she made some cost saving suggestions, then finally said: When this is all over send us a bill and we'll write a cheque. Of course, we had no idea then what the final tally would be.

Marcia spoke with the eye surgeon who wanted consent to remove my eye. It was in fact almost removed already: it was lying on my upper cheek still attached only by the optical nerve. Somehow that didn't upset her but she was very emotional about the removal and asked if we could wait to see if there would be any improvement or recovery. She was told no; the damaged eye would affect sight in the other eye and that it had to come out, the sooner the better. Fortunately for her we were evacuated the next day, the surgery was done in Australia and she didn't have to consent. She was so afraid of me being angry with her for having my eye removed.

On December 15 we were flown to Australia. The locals had retrieved our wallets and passports and had packed a bag of clothes for each of us. I was taken to the airport by ambulance and Marcia was driven in a car. I was in a hospital gown; Marcia was given a white eyelet nightgown, fortunately full length, and a sun hat. She still had no idea how badly bruised she was or that she had 3 lines of stitches in her head.

When we arrived at the airport the pilot was anxious to leave as it was getting dark. We were accompanied by a man in full fire suit, another man, possibly a co-pilot, and a female medical attendant who said that she would monitor me and that Marcia should relax, which she did, falling asleep almost immediately. We had to fly at sea level to reduce the risk of any additional swelling of my brain so it was a long flight requiring a refuelling stop in Port Moresby. We landed in Cairns, the closest immigration office to PNG. All formalities were taken care of for us as we transferred to the hospital by ambulance. The admitting doctor explained that I would be in intensive care for the night, that we would transfer to the larger regional hospital in Townsville in the morning, and that Marcia was discharged. As it was the middle of the night, she had no money and was wearing only a nightgown, she opted to stay in the hospital and went to the waiting room to try to sleep on a rattan couch. A nurse saw her, said I think we can give you a bed and found an empty one.

At some point Marcia had to use the washroom and got her first glimpse of herself. Her head was shaved with stitches in three places that looked like 100-pound test fishing line. She had huge bruises around each eye and down her cheeks to her mouth. She was quite shocked at her appearance, as she had no idea that she had a head injury as well. No one had ever told her about her condition, or if they had she didn't comprehend it.

The next morning we flew to Townsville with the Flying Doctor. As we left the airplane Marcia asked how we would be billed and was told the Flying Doctor never charges, a wonderful service. Unfortunately, the ambulance and the air ambulance both did, as well as the Australian and Canadian hospitals.

Once again I was admitted to intensive care and Marcia was discharged. This time she asked to see a doctor as she had some problems: the worst headache of her life and restricted vision in her left eye. She says it was like looking through and around a doughnut. A CT scan revealed a skull fracture and bruising on her brain as well so she was admitted to the room next to me.

Although she was once again hooked up to an IV pole she was mobile and could visit me at will. She had a fever so was not allowed too many blankets and was always cold. My temperature was low so I was regularly given heated blankets so she often climbed in with me, as it felt so warm and cozy.

While in the Intensive Care Unit I finally woke up from my coma, and as I did, I improved quickly. No longer had just my life become changed forever but many changes were made as well to Marcia's life, creating burdens for her that lasted for some time. My son Michael arrived in Townsville shortly after we were admitted. He was given the details of my condition and consented to the eye surgery.

The doctors felt that I was progressing much faster than expected so I moved into the head injury unit, which I guess meant I was doing very well. Michael came daily to help me shower, shave, dress, and then spent the day with me. I could move around and sit up giving me a bit more comfort. My head was still very badly damaged from the eight skull fractures. The doctors could not, of course, guarantee the outcome of my recovery but surprisingly I had recognized my son and this impressed them. However, there was no way to know how much I would recover. No one could know.

Chapter 11

Australia Hospital

I T IS NOW DECEMBER 21. Today I was able to communicate with Michael for the first time. I don't know if I made much sense but at least it was a beginning. I started to spend as much time as I could standing and holding on to the bed to build strength in my legs. All I know is that I have to be strong again. Maybe I can't do all the other things I did before but at least I will run again. Of that I had no doubt in my mind.

December 22 was my birthday but I had no idea what that meant. Visitors from the Townsville sailing community and the hospital came by to celebrate. I was able to sit up but was totally confused by all the action. I was completely unable to make any sense of the voices and was unable to speak or think with any clarity. I didn't know what was wrong with me but I knew that something terrible had happened. That evening Marcia received several email birthday greetings for me from friends and my children back home. Again, I was not able to speak anything that made sense. I felt very depressed and again knew that something really terrible had happened to me. In spite of my inability to speak, my confusion showed through and I cried.

Those few days were terribly depressing to me. Just waking up enough to realize the enormity of the difficulties I had made me sad. I could see nothing that made sense. I could speak nothing that made sense. I felt worthless and yet I knew that I had been someone in the past. But for now I even felt less than a nobody, I felt worthless. In fact when I lay at night I thought of who I had been, who I was now, what have I become, what will I ever be able to do again? Can I ever be a normal human being again? You can't ask those questions without also asking the other half of the question, Why am I still alive? and I could never ask that about dying. So every day I tried to look forward to my better side, making my life, hanging on to the good side.

One of the hospital therapists came to see me for an afternoon. She spent quite a bit of time talking to me, asking where I had been, who I was, what I could understand. She showed me pictures to identify. Was that a cup? What is that, a glass? Was that a house? I could not understand anything. I think in the deep recesses of my mind I felt something and knew something was in there but I could not get thoughts and words out so I became very angry. The therapist ended my session at this point and said we would carry on the next day. The following day Marcia came to visit with me while the therapist was working with me. I didn't want Marcia to witness my embarrassment and my total inability, so I told her to go away, making her cry. I guess everybody pays a price along the way when misfortune happens.

The therapist started again. "Can you say these words? Can you tell me what these blocks of coloured words mean? Can you understand what this means?" Once again I was asked for answers that I could not give. I could understand almost nothing. Frustration again overwhelmed me. I think the therapist eventually gave up on me as each time I became so frustrated at not being able to give at least a few answers. I guess my brain cells were not going to respond. I did learn a few things slowly on my own in spite of the therapist. I have no doubt she had good intentions but for the frustration that I felt then; I know what I would like to do with that cup or that glass.

I started to eat meals on my own. This was a way to find

out who I am and I was determined to do it on my own. I don't think it went well but each time I learned and improved. In the beginning it was rather funny, I'm sure, for the nurses. I ate granola with my fingers, drinking the milk out of the bowl, spilling some over me. I ate jam with a spoon as my body craved sweets, something I never ate before. My toast I handled with my hands, adding on more jam. I had no idea how to eat meat with a knife and fork so I stabbed it and ate around the edges. This was sure turning into a new and strange world. I couldn't remember how to do the simplest things. Using a toilet when you can't remember having ever seen one before was totally mystifying so I always needed help. When Michael showed me how to brush my teeth I started off reasonably OK but then I carried on brushing outside my lips and along my face. Each day I had to learn a new thing and a new idea. My brain learned quickly but not as fast as I wanted. Michael helped me so much and I knew I was improving, but I couldn't help building up anxiety about myself and also occasional anger about my situation.

On December 25, Christmas Day, Michael and Marcia came to the hospital early to spend the whole day with me. I was doing quite well and progressing slightly but I'm not sure my vocabulary was increasing. I kept saying "Where are the people, what about my people, shall we send a list to the people or will we be going there?" Was this my way of telling myself something about Christmas? I really don't know. Michael and Marcia never did determine what I was talking about, they just learned to agree with me.

As the coffee shop was closed that day Marcia brought food for herself and Michael, then they were served leftover dinners, as many patients were out for the day so we all had lots to eat. My eating habits were getting back to normal, however, the milk was still usually spilt. Scrambled eggs were easiest to eat with a spoon and fingers.

I was trying to walk to recover my strength with Michael

helping me. I wanted to walk by myself but hospital staff insisted that was impossible. I was required to wear a vest with straps and handles on each side for someone to hold onto for support or to grab to prevent me from falling, which at least allowed me to take a few walks. In my mind I was determined to run again. Michael kept telling me that I would get better again but at this stage I didn't even want to think about it. I felt that I might never be able to speak again, read again, make music again, but in my heart at least I knew I would run again. Why? I was already walking, although a bit shaky. After a few days of the vest I was allowed to willingly pass it on to the next recipient as I progressed to getting support by leaning on the wall, with help when needed by Michael or Marcia. Before long I was supporting myself. My unsteadiness continued for a while and someone was always watching me but my strength grew very quickly and my eyes lit up with every step I made as I kept increasing my distance.

By December 29 I was walking all the time and getting stronger. I even strolled outdoors. It was very warm and it must have brought reminiscence to my mind of sailing the boat in New Zealand. Now I stop and think Where is my boat? I can't even remember the name of it, or where it is, my mind is blank. In spite of these problems I have been getting much better daily. Michael continually asks the doctors to set a date for us all to return to Canada so that I can recover at home.

Finally the doctors agree, everything is arranged and we are ready to leave. Thinking about flying to Canada is exciting but the connection from Australia through New Zealand and Los Angeles is a bit daunting to my mind. Not only that but I am still not clear about what happened to my boat or to me and about leaving the boat in Rabaul unattended. I had recovered so much in such a short period of time at this hospital and still I was at the beginning stage of the work ahead. Amazing what our bodies can handle, what life gives to us; yet we survive.

Rio Nimpkish in Blue Mouse Cove

Saying goodbye to our friends

A good day at sea

A hard day at work

Up a tree in Toau, Tuamotu Islands, French Polynesia

Taking a camel to dinner, Alice Springs, Australia

One of our dancing girls from Maupiti

Some of the kids having fun as usual in Maupiti

Local dancing in Atutaki, Cook Islands

Giant Kauri tree stump, New Zealand

A quiet day at sea

A not so quiet day

Cross Country, Brisbane 2001 before my accident

Rabaul market

Simpson Harbour, Rabaul, Namanula Hill is on the left

My son Michael getting me ready to leave Townsville hospital

My first race after my accident 2002 TC10K I walked

Ed and Michelle's wedding day

The day *Rio Nimpkish* came back

Chapter 12

Gorge Road Hospital

ON JANUARY 7 AT 6 AM we flew from Townsville to Brisbane, then to Auckland where we spent the night. The next day we flew to Los Angeles, Vancouver, and then finally the short flight to Victoria. Michael's wife Karen met us at the Vancouver airport with my two grandsons. We arrived in Victoria in the evening and were met by my brother who drove me directly to Victoria General Hospital. At the admission desk I knew my name, address, telephone number, and that I had worked in that hospital for many years. Later I forgot this information and had to learn it again.

For the first few days I was not allowed to leave my room and all visitors had to be gowned and masked due to quarantine isolation. Very soon though I moved to a room in the head injury ward: my home for the next month or so. After several appointments with an eye specialist I was able to have a prosthetic eye fitted. I was also able to leave the hospital for a few hours for lunch or supper.

Finally, after about 5 weeks, I transferred to the Gorge Road Rehabilitation Hospital, which became my home for several months. I felt safe. Walls and windows surrounded me. I could feel the wind drift by as the doors opened often. There were large beautiful trees to the side and in the distance I could glimpse the blue sea passing by. Also, the birds nearby added their beauty.

Once I settled in, my therapy began in earnest. All of us in the ward woke up in time for a shower early in the morning. I don't think things vary too much between kids and adults racing each other except our situation was a little bit different involving our physical problems: damaged legs, arms, heads or whatever; carts, wheels, walkers and everything else we needed made it more difficult to rush off to the shower. Well, you win some and you lose some but I was getting pretty fast on my feet so in that department I was making good headway and was often first.

I didn't feel as if my speech was picking up any, but at least I progressed in other ways. My breakfast always tasted great to me. Then I could go for a walk; this I looked forward to, the activity that kept me going when I couldn't do anything else. I thought I might never be able to do useful things again but this I was sure of: I would run again. So I started out every day for my walk. Someone had to accompany me in the beginning but as I continued to improve I had more license to add distance, until eventually I got once around the building. Naturally the next trip would be two times around the building, trying to do it faster. Recklessness doesn't always seem like recklessness at the time and I felt in control of the situation. I had suffered some seizures due to my head injury, but only a few, and was warned that running could contribute to one. I didn't want to create any problems that might interfere with my recovery but I was starting to feel good about myself, so I started some short jogging runs in the back of the hospital which was less visible to the staff. I guess this could be taken as a bit of dishonesty but seeing no improvement in my music, speaking or reading, I was willing to take a chance on having a seizure. What did I have to lose? It was important to me to know that I could become independent and strong again; that was what my running meant to me.

After my walk I went back to school. Each patient in his own way had to relearn how to speak, how to act, how to be himself again. We were all mixed up in some way. Some were injured in an accident, struck by a vehicle of some sort, some at work, many by a stroke, some in a fight, and some on a construction site. Many things cause head injuries. One moment we are in perfect shape, walking, talking, running, working, seeing our friends and families, living our lives. Then in a moment our lives changed. How could this happen so quickly? It's too immense, too impossible to understand. I'm sure this is why our minds can relearn things and that we are open and ready when it's our time.

Daily I continued to work, playing games, using books and learning words that I used to know before but that now were new strange things. I also had to learn how to use a computer, which is nothing new for kids, but for me it was a difficult chore that I had to try to teach my less nimble brain. But day by day I kept working and eventually things would brighten up to another level, and those were the things that kept me going.

I remember another patient who I will call Mabel. She was a retired schoolteacher who had difficulty speaking and walking after a stroke so used a wheelchair. Her injuries caused problems for her learning to read and speak, as did mine, but she made up for it with her great sense of humour. After supper I generally had studying to do from my day work. While passing her room I asked Mabel if she would like to join me to study. She readily agreed, so I pushed her chair to a comfortable area where we could work. One particular day we were each given several stories which were missing words. It was up to us to read the stories and replace the blank spaces with words. We took a turn as to who was the reader and who would choose the missing word. It started out being a serious job each time we wrote out appropriate letters to fill the blank spaces but it became quite a chore. However, Mabel started laughing at one rather funny story about fishing. I, a good east coaster from Nova Scotia, added my two bits worth of humour trying to say something about the squid jigging ground, but of course with my head injury I couldn't say it the right way. So between her stroke and my head injury, the funnier it got and the more foolish we became. This carried on back and forth several times until it became quite funny.

We continued working together for a while. Later she was transferred to another hospital so I never saw her again, but we did have a lot of fun while it lasted. I guess in a way we were both misfits but I felt in relatively good shape because I could walk. I suppose she felt better off because she could speak better than I could. We enjoyed our conversation several times a day. Friendships have a way of happening by themselves. The less you do to prepare it the more comfortable it becomes. I think that happens with children but as we grow older we somehow develop protections to keep our distance, to be safe. And in truth, safety costs us a price. When Mabel left I was saddened, but I understood, like others, that this was just another way to develop emotional protection that I had to relearn. Even as children we have to learn about loss and pain, and as we continue to grow we learn how to protect ourselves from adversity. As adults, we have to deal with the pain of loss and protect ourselves from adversity but still reach out to people who might leave us behind.

My friend Ed was getting married. I had known him for many years from our work at Victoria General Hospital and from crewing on my sailboat. I didn't know the date of his wedding, but I knew it would still be a while before I would be well enough to join in on any activities with him. That day during our rest time, which was generally a quiet time, I was lying on my bed when a great sound of voices came towards me, saying someone wanted to see me. I opened my eyes and several people appeared, smiling and looking very happy about something. Then in front of my eyes appeared Ed wearing a beautifully fitted tux. I had forgotten what something like that even looked like. Alongside was his new wife, Michelle, so wide-eyed and beautiful in her new gown. It was really a sight to see. Ed and Michelle posed for pictures with me and we had some time together. Their visit was short as it was meant to be, but it was very special for me to be included in their day. Youth and beauty always make us happy and it certainly did that afternoon for everyone there. For the rest of us old guys wearing old dressing gowns in the background, I don't think the Gorge Road Hospital will be quite the same ever again.

Chapter 13

Red Tomatoes

T ODAY WAS GOING TO be a big day for me. I was going to go to a supermarket for the first time since my head injury. I wasn't sure what I was going to do but I was always anxious to learn about new things. Betty (the therapist) told me that I was going to go to the shopping centre, get some groceries, and then come back home for our lunch. Well, I thought, what is new about that? We have our food given to us every day at the hospital. So we started off to the shopping centre. She told me to stay with her and to enjoy the experience. Without a doubt it was quite an experience, nothing that I expected.

It was so overwhelming for me that it is impossible for me to explain. I felt like I was in a new world. I'm sure a new-born child must feel the same emotions when her mother gives her bright colourful toys for the first time. There were colours I had never seen before, there were things of all sizes and descriptions I had never imagined before, there were smells I had never smelled before; so many people around doing things together. There were bright lights blinking, sounds that scared me, people everywhere. Someone would ring a bell to signal somebody to carry something away, and then another bell would ring for something else going on. To me it seemed total confusion. I felt that my mind was going to come apart in pieces.

What did give me some enjoyment with its beauty were all the colourful fruit and vegetables everywhere imaginable. There were piles upon piles, row upon row, colour upon colour: red, yellow, green, orange, purple, everything you could imagine. You could smell them and you could touch them. I had never seen anything like it. And yet, no one but me seemed to notice the produce or what was going on. I felt then they really were real. It was time to go now.

I stayed close to Betty as we came to the cash register so that she could show me how to pay for our items with some money. I was nervous. I just wanted to be back home. Everything seemed to bother me all of a sudden as I started back to the Gorge carrying the vegetables. We walked part-way home when suddenly everything began to overwhelm me. I thought of all the trouble I had been having with my lack of ability to speak and my lost ability to play music. I had been fighting myself. I was angry as well over my lack of ability to read. It all seemed too much for me to deal with. I walked over to the side of the street and found some quiet grass and trees along which I sat down. From there Betty knew I could get back by myself.

How long I stayed there I don't know but it seemed forever. I could only think of myself. How could I ever be me again? My eyes welled up: I closed my eyes and I cried. I had always held tears back but my emotions were too real now. I was desperate. Then slowly, one moment at a time, something began to happen. I became angry, and as my anger grew I grew with it. With my running I was always able to fight my way back from a walk to a run. I was not going to let the guy in Papua New Guinea who beat me up stop me from carrying on with my life. And as fast as the anger came it changed, and I began to feel strong and alive again. This will be just one more step of many. I walked the rest of the way back home feeling much better about myself.

I looked at the vegetables in the bag that I was carrying, beautiful with their lush colours. I picked up the big red tomatoes. Why had I never really seen them before?

Chapter 14

Dealing with Everyday Life

MY WORK AT THE Gorge Road Hospital was designed to teach me how to function in and be useful to the community again. In the beginning I didn't see any changes but gradually, as I grew stronger, I began to feel that I might become a normal person again. That was a good feeling and although I didn't feel that way all of the time that was all right, because I knew that everything was improving. I also had no illusions about my abilities or myself but everything I was learning helped me to move forward; this was always greatly exciting for me.

I had been at the Gorge for some time and had recovered to the point where I could spend a night at our home with Marcia. This would be my first day and night away from the Gorge. After breakfast as I was relaxing and daydreaming, waiting for Marcia to pick me up my daydreaming brought me back to my exciting sailing days, how easily I could sail single-handed, even climb the mast by myself. There was not one part of the sailing gear that I couldn't handle with my eyes closed, even under water if I had to. Oh, but for those days. They seem so long ago.

I talked to Marcia on the phone for a while: How are things? Are the flowers growing? And so on. The bathroom faucet leaks she said. Should I call a plumber? No, let me look at it first

I said. Why, I practically rebuilt part of this house over the last 20 years I mumbled to myself. She picked me up and brought me to our house for my overnight stay. I got out of the car and walked around. The house looked so big now. I hardly remembered it, I can barely remember the last time I was here.

No question about it, my security now comes from sleeping at the Gorge. We looked at the yard, the flowers and the trees. The whole house was quite beautiful but it quietly scared me. I couldn't explain why and I still can't, except to say that I was in a new-to-me, environment. I was still not ready for and not able to cope with anything new. I came inside with Marcia and had some tea while we talked about the house and my grandchildren. They are always a joy to talk about regarding who is doing this and that and their latest news. It was good.

By the way, honey, what is the problem with the leak? We need a new faucet. All of my good quality tools were stolen from the boat in Papua New Guinea, but I still had lots of older gear here if only I still know how to use it. Hmm, hmm. I put the light on the problem and thought about it for a while. I tried again in a different way but it didn't work any better. This was always so simple before, nothing at all to it, what is going wrong? Nevertheless, I kept at it in spite of the fact that it was not going right. I tried several ways that didn't work. Try and try again, but the leak kept showing.

I worked for several hours. I was very frustrated, this was supposed to be a quick job after which Marcia and I could spend the rest of the day enjoying ourselves. After all, this was my first day at home from the hospital and I was supposed to be enjoying it. Eventually I got some other tools together and was able to make the leak stop. However, I was not completely convinced that the repair was perfect, so I didn't feel good about it.

By now Marcia was also upset about everything as well. She was making dinner for the two of us and here I was spending all afternoon taking so much time to do one little job. It was all too much. I couldn't handle it! It seemed to blow up all at once. I guess when you are over the edge your brain has different ways of thinking how it should act. My day off was enough. I wanted to get out of here, to go back "home" which in my mind was the Gorge where I had my bed. I walked out, closed the door and left.

I'll find my own way I said to myself. This was a bad thing for me to do by myself for this would be my first time alone downtown since my head injury. I'll worry about that as I go along I thought. I'm sure I'll recognize something that I remember along the way. I kept walking but things didn't seem to make sense to me. I knew that I had been in this area many times but now nothing looked familiar and I just couldn't decide which way I should go. I was feeling a little bit nervous but then I turned a different direction and sure enough, to my side was water. I knew that the Gorge was along the water so I naturally headed in that direction.

Unfortunately, the Gorge wasn't just sitting there waiting for me to arrive straightforward; but with a lot of walking and asking questions I kept the water on my left, and eventually I could see our building. Already the security of my room was beginning to envelop me. I came through the parking lot into the front door. Marcia was waiting for me! She was crying and then I felt terrible about it all. But through it all, what can you do about things that happen to you, you have to just carry on with your life and move on to the next step. A great percentage of relationships fail in the first year or two after a head injury, because people are not able to cope with the stress that builds up in their lives.

I had been at the Gorge for some time but I often stopped to think about what had happened to me. My memory often brought back glimpses of the hospital in Australia. I thought back to how I must have spent my time, trying to understand who I was, what happened to me, and who I had become. Michael and Marcia both came to the hospital in Townsville at different times, to be with me all day: for breakfast or later for a walk. There were so many things I wanted to be able to say but because of my head injury I was unable to speak or to show my feelings. I know that they had both set up Christmas dinner for me with gifts, but I had no idea what it all meant at that time. Now it would be very special.

I know they were waiting for the month to pass for my body to heal, so that we all could fly back home to Canada to see our families. How wonderful if only they could have had Christmas dinner with their families in their own homes, but of course that was not possible. Yes, we who have serious injuries to deal with can survive, and we do, and thankfully we usually have someone to help us. But sometimes we forget that there are others who pay a price as well for the hardships that come with taking care of friends and families dear to us.

Today I was going to see Alison, a therapist, to talk about how I was feeling about some problems. It was kind of funny for me to feel upset, for all my life I thought of myself as being a regular, normal guy, but now without question my life had certainly changed.

My session this day was to help me deal with the problems I was experiencing over my seizures and how I felt about them, and to help me deal with my unusual melancholy or depression. This was not something that I had experienced in my past; it cropped up since my head injury. My running not only helped to keep me in shape but it also gave me an uplift of good feelings afterwards. Lately though this had not been happening; my usual sense of fulfilment was not there. So today I was going to see Alison. I set out with plenty of time to spare for my two o'clock meeting.

On the way I passed a little shop which I had never stopped to look at. Maybe the look might not be beautiful in the front but oh – the aroma was so delicious! I got a whiff of it as I passed by the door and had to go in, as I had plenty of time to spare. To the left was the main purchasing area where several people were buying bags of bread with the familiar cash register merrily jingling. Along with bags of bread were the usual candies, cakes and knickknacks. To the right were four small comfortable tables where I plopped myself down for a cup of tea to relax, look at the excitement, and smell the aroma.

This is the sort of thing I like. I think my brain must work like sponges to just absorb everything it needs whenever it wants it. It seems that some days I get a bite in my mind as if it were the first time I had seen something and yet I know that would not be correct. It's sort of deja vu. Perhaps on the right day in the right circumstances we can change. For today, the aroma was tantalizing. I don't remember being in a bakery with so many smells and so many different seeds that looked like peanuts or sesame seeds, all looking exotic. I suppose for anyone else it was just another regular shop, but for me it was something new again. "Charlie! There's a big yellow bag in the back room. We need the pumpernickel bread right away!" someone said. I shook my head. Damn! I looked at my watch. It was almost two o'clock. How did the time go so fast? I was going to have to rush very fast to be on time for my meeting. So much for giving myself plenty of time to spare.

Chapter 15

Dealing with Seizures

W HEN WE FEEL AS if our survival is threatened we will take a beating if we must to protect ourselves, but as we become more secure we want to make sure that we don't lose what we already have. I had been discharged from the Gorge for a few weeks and was doing quite well. I had not had a seizure for a few months. This in itself gave me a lot of confidence but I guess overconfidence affected my running. I was not thinking about seizures and had not developed any ideas about what might prevent one while I was running. Since then, I have become more practical and have developed safeguards to help me be more conscious of my running habits.

Unfortunately, at that time I was by myself and not properly prepared, as I would be now. I don't know for sure what happened to me that day but I believe that the traffic was part of it; too many cars and too many people gave me the confusion that caused a seizure. In any case I became quite mixed up, going without control in strange and different directions; then I remember falling down. When I woke up I was in some bushes. I don't know how long I lay there but when I woke I could walk although I did have pain in my shoulder. It turned out that I broke my collarbone in the fall. Although I was a bit groggy I found my way, and walked the rest of the way home. I decided then that it would be better not to run alone. I kept that up for a long time even as I once again started to feel stronger and was no longer having any seizures.

By May 2005 I hadn't had a seizure for 2 years. I almost felt as if I was immune to the darn things but I would never go so far as to be that foolish. I had been taking good care of myself, doing all the things I felt I should be doing when this seizure came totally out of the blue. It's hard to believe that it could happen so fast. It came upon me very rapidly and within an hour or so I was wrapped up in a grand mal seizure.

I had been running very well and was absolutely not aware of any problem of any nature. I was with friends, who were also good runners, on a bright, sunny and warm day around 10 AM I had picked up my pace a bit for about a mile. I was about three-quarters of my way through the run when I started feeling strange. Then I started stumbling and running in odd directions. I didn't know where I was going and became totally confused. I stopped, closed my eyes until I could walk again, then I felt better. I walked for a bit, then tried running to see what would happen. I seemed to be able to hang on for a moment but not for long as once again I became overwhelmed by the bright sunshine and by a confusion I couldn't control. In the heat I had taken my cap off. If only I had worn it I might have protected my eyes from the brightness and myself from the seizure. Later I learned how to deal with this. What caused my problem on this particular trail was the bright light intermittent with the dark shadows of big trees. The flickering between the two was the problem.

By now my friends had caught up to me and realized that I was in some difficulty. They helped me back to our car. My confusion and dizziness increased as my condition deteriorated to the point that my hand began to tremble. A friend drove us to the hospital where I immediately saw a physician who, realizing I was having a grand mal seizure, set up intravenous medication for me. Trying to control myself became more difficult until very quickly, I lost control of my right hand, which was by now shaking. I knew what was coming next and I couldn't stop it as the light began to dim and my whole head went grey.

When I woke my arms and legs were sore from fighting back. I had also bitten my lip in spite of the protection I was given to prevent that. I spent that day and the next resting, remembering again who I was and being angry about everything, about having to start over again, rebuilding my brain cells again for a month or so to where I was previously. I was very angry in the beginning but I didn't allow anger to control me beyond that point or it would have become my enemy and no longer of any use to me. So slowly I continued working hard and within two or three months had returned to my previous level of ability, as well as learning the new habits, which I developed into my seizure plan.

You might say: Why run at all? Why risk creating a problem that might cause a seizure when you don't need to? With a small degree of politeness I would agree. But without my independence and fortitude I would not have realized why my seizures were happening. I would love to say that they will never happen again, but of course that is not possible to suggest. All I can say is that I hope to continue running seizure free for many years to come. Just like some people love to golf, others like me love to run. It gives me a lift, a joy that makes me feel good, and it is a big reason why we meet our friends.

Running has been a joy for me for many, many years. A side effect of running has been to help me to recover and to learn my music. I am quite convinced that my head injury improved greatly due to the maximum use of my body in physical exercise. Exercise is very good therapy and I think it helps to bring oxygen to our body to help us work better. I find when my running improves my reading slightly improves. Without a doubt I have improved in being able to make a little bit of music again.

In August 2005 I went to Duncan to compete in several races at the BC Seniors Games. This is a large three-day event with a gala dinner as the main event one evening. Marcia and I met some friends and were seated in our designated area. The food was beautifully catered in spite of the size of the building, a hockey arena, which was large enough to accommodate everyone. We were sitting with a group enjoying our meal when I began to feel strangeness in my head, nothing that I could pinpoint or speak about to anybody. Inwardly though I knew something was happening to me and it was not good.

Then in a split second I realized what was happening. Directly over my head was a strobe light. The on and off flickering contrast of black and white light in my eyes was setting me up for a seizure. This was what I had felt without realizing it. You never saw anyone move as fast as I did until I found a quiet area where there were no bright lights above me. It turned out that several other people had problems as well, and asked to have the strobe light turned off.

Since then I have developed a plan for preventing or avoiding seizures:

Always tell another person where you will be going
Always wear a wristband showing your medical alert number
Run with someone if possible
Wear a hat or visor to protect your eye from bright light
Wear proper glasses for sun protection
Stay well away from strobe or flashing lights
Try to avoid areas of high contrast – shadows in bright sunlight, for example
Always be properly hydrated before running
Always eat properly before running
And for anyone moving from running to cycling, don't forget your helmet!

Other ideas are also helpful but these are the main points that stand out to me.

Chapter 16

Return to Rabaul

A S I RECOVERED I became concerned about how to have *Rio Nimpkish* returned to Canada. We investigated several possibilities: shipping the boat from Rabaul to somewhere in Australia, the South Pacific or even the North American west coast; or hiring a captain to sail it to Australia or North America. All avenues seemed too difficult and were too expensive. Then two sailing friends, David and Paul, offered to sail the boat home to Victoria for me. David took his son James as additional crew. Marcia organized their trip and flew back to Rabaul with David and James to prepare the boat. Paul joined them a few days later.

On May 2, 2002 they left. Marcia had been advised by email from the local yacht club that the boat had been broken into twice despite the security measures in place. She was in close contact to determine what equipment had been stolen as it would have to be replaced in Victoria and taken along as there was no place in Rabaul to buy such things. David and Paul took some of their own boat equipment and we purchased additional safety items. Organizing gear in the last few days before the trip was a frantic time for Marcia as some items such as safety flares couldn't be taken on a commercial flight.

After a long flight through Honolulu, Sidney, Cairns and Port Moresby to Rabaul, they arrived around 5:30 PM, almost dark, with no one to meet them as arranged. A local who was picking up his wife offered them a ride to a nearby town; then ended up driving them all the way to Rabaul.

The next day they met one of the yacht club members who had been looking after the boat, who gave them the boat keys and loaned them the yacht club dinghy. Poor *Rio Nimpkish*. What a mess! He had bashed into a mooring ball for 5 months so the new paint job from New Zealand was chipped. He was filthy, covered in volcano dust, sulphur corrosion and red stains. Betel (a nut chewed for a mild narcotic buzz) juice? As Marcia emptied a couple of lockers for James and David to use and started to pack up our things, the extent of the thefts amazed her. All of our clothes were stolen, our jewellery, our running gear, her art supplies, my saxophone, our cassette tapes and CDs, the stereo, small appliances, and dishes. We had had enough camping gear to hike totally self-sufficiently, but all that was left in the camping locker was a short bungy cord. She started to cry. "I wonder why they didn't take this?" "Because it's too short to be of any use," said the ever practical David. The lovely Christmas present she had bought, wrapped and hidden, boxes of food, items bought for trading in the islands, even our photos were all gone.

They quickly established a routine; David sorted boat supplies to see what was on board and what was needed. James cooked fabulous vegetarian meals. When Paul arrived he checked boat systems. Marcia packed items to bring home or to ship. She was very upset by the condition of the boat and knew how enraged I would be if I saw the mess.

With the men ashore shopping, she spent much of the first days sobbing. The mess didn't improve with David and James buying more gear and trying to settle in as she packed.

The shipping agent, Peter Cohen, was wonderful: he took Marcia under his wing, gave her coffee, let her use his office email, and took her home for lunch. He was also shocked by the way the boat had been maintained, and by the thefts.

Someone provided a cardboard shipping carton, which he declared unacceptable, and had his carpenter rebuild. His wife Julie drove Marcia to the police station to report the missing items as well as she could remember. The police had my saxophone and some cassette tapes waiting to be identified and claimed. They promised a report for insurance purposes, which never materialized, but they did show more interest when they saw that one of the stolen items was a gun. It was just a pellet gun but it got their attention.

Marcia packed everything she wanted to ship into the new crate and delivered it to the shipping office. The customs office waived the inspection fees and the shipping company waived their portion of shipping costs, cheering up Marcia with their generosity. Everyone on the island had heard about our attack. The brutality shocked them and they wanted to help however they could.

Julie took Marcia to the hospital to pay our bill. The accountant couldn't find it so she paid it again: 88 kina or about $30 for a 3 night stay for 2 people, one in intensive care. The security guard that was paid to sleep on our boat wrote Marcia a note asking for more money, as the job was so dangerous. As he was a hotel employee, on hearing this the manager of the hotel, who was also a yacht club official, beat him; supposedly on her behalf. She was so outraged that she could barely speak. She was not able to tell some of the local whites what she thought of their racist ways as David and Paul still needed a lot of help and local information to get the boat ready. As it was, they all got a very cool reception.

Marcia packed as many bags as she could to bring home with her while the men asked her questions about the boat systems. Peter and Julie arranged for her to stay with a friend who lived close to the airport and drove her there for her early morning flight. After another long trip in reverse, she arrived back in Victoria.

Chapter 17

Rio Nimpkish Returns

WHILE THEY WERE SAILING back to Victoria I was thinking about *Rio Nimpkish*, David, Paul and Jamie. "I wonder where they are. I worry a lot about their location. Are they OK? Are they encountering any storms? When will they arrive?" I can't help but think that I should be the one sailing the boat but I know that is not possible for me to do now. I have learned that I am no longer capable of handling the things I could in the past. I will say that I still have times of sadness and of missing the past, my sailing and my adventures. But for the most part I am quite content to have had the incredible time I had travelling around the world.

In spite of the pain of rehabilitation that I had to go through, I look at my last few years as a blessing in disguise. I have no regrets. In fact, I often look at myself now as being a better person than I was before. I am not sure why that should be – I had everything I ever wanted before but now those things don't seem as important as they did. Just a simple new day is special to me now. Never before would I have ever looked at a dandelion as being beautiful but now I have actually stopped to see one. Every day seems to be more beautiful than it was before. Like my music, beauty comes back to me and gives me a lot of help in setting my priorities and purposes. Dealing with my near death experience has helped me. It has brought me closer to others in ways of compassion and understanding that I never had before. I think this has made me a better person.

The phone rang. *Rio Nimpkish* had arrived in Victoria. It was in the harbour; all the crew had arrived safe and sound. Has a new life begun? I don't think so. We just move on to something else, maybe bigger or better, maybe the same, but the important thing is that we carry on with new excitement that keeps us going.

Epilogue

WHENEVER I THOUGHT ABOUT the incident, I had a keen desire to tell what had happened to me. I wanted to show that I would be myself again. However, my ability to speak was negligible, and until now I had not done any writing. As a child I always enjoyed reading and writing, and was generally good at it. So now, after all these years, I decided to try it again.

I knew what I wanted to say, but I had to transpose my thinking into words on paper. I could always do it before, but could I do it now? I tried and, surprisingly enough, it worked! I was able to write just as I always could. I guess my brain activity in that area was not damaged. However, each time I tried to read and understand what I had just written, I could not make sense of it.

What I wrote was done properly, and Marcia would read it and say that it was fine, but my eye-brain connection was the problem. This connection couldn't be fixed immediately or easily, but with hard work, over time my learning abilities improved markedly. I know that I will always have some problems with writing and reading, but at least now I feel that it is manageable and I can survive with it.

Day by day I challenge myself to become more aware and alive to the world around me. My music has improved in great bounds. I had to learn all about flats, sharps, musical notes and how to read music all over again, but the sounds came back more easily. Now I play my saxophone at our Christmas party.

I had to sell my boat as it was too much for me to handle, but now I have a kayak that I use on my own. I ride my bicycle safely around the city and I arrange my own transportation from Victoria to Vancouver and back on the ferry.

I am running again and competing in races. I always have difficulty knowing the number of laps on the track, as I never know for sure which one I have completed but fortunately others around me realize the problem and make sure to tell me when I am ready to finish a race. In August of 2006 I competed in the BC Seniors Games, winning 2 gold and 4 silver medals in my category.

For those who think that life is over after adversity, think again. Never give up for it is the most beautiful experience that you can have. Never give it away, as it is special. Keep working towards it. You may have problems and difficulties. You may even think that you have insurmountable problems –but you can still work them out.

My best to you and good luck.

With that I leave you with:

Thanks

Humility

Courage and

Red Tomatoes

Attacker Jailed for 20 Years

THE NATIONAL COURT IN Kokopo has jailed a young man, who took out his frustration by assaulting two foreigners in Rabaul last year, for 20 years with hard labour. And the East New Britain Chamber of Commerce and Industry has applauded the decision. But Chamber president David Loh has reminded tourists and others that the incident was a one-off and did not reflect the behaviour and attitudes of the peace-loving East New Britain people.

Dadly Gorop Henry, 21, of Rabaul, pleaded guilty to a charge that on December 11, 2001 at Namanul Hill, Rabaul, he stole with actual violence from two expatriate tourists, James Leslie MacNeill and Olivia Marcia Stromsmoe, two cameras and K150 in cash. The couple, from Canada, sailed into Rabaul on their 39-ft yacht to repair minor damage to the yacht. They had been living in Rabaul for several days and on that fateful day, they decided to walk up the Namanula Hill lookout. According to the police brief, Henry became their guide and led them from the Kaivuna Motel up the Namanula road.

Henry took the couple to the old premier's residence site where he attacked them, using a tree branch to hit them until they became unconscious. The accused took the cameras and cash. A medical report from the Townsville General Hospital presented in court confirmed several head injuries suffered by both victims. Mr MacNeill had bruising and laceration on the left side of his scalp, his left eye was ruptured and torn and an X-ray scan showed multiple skull fractures and other injuries. Ms Stromsmoe also suffered extensive head injuries and fractures to one of her eyes and was unable to see properly.

The attack stirred anger among the business community and residents of Rabaul town who took it on themselves to look for the assailant. Henry allegedly joined in the search, riding on the back of one of the vehicles to Matupit Island following a lead on the attacker. The search team approached a youth, who pointed out Henry.

Justice Salateil Lenalia told Henry that what he did not only hurt the victims, but brought great shame to Papua New Guinea and was bad for the tourism industry in the country. "You took advantage of the two foreigners being unarmed, being away from their homeland and their people and committed this serious crime on them," Justice Lenalia said. "Your case paints a bad picture to the tourism industry in this country. In any case, all Papua New Guineans should feel responsible when we have visitors visiting our towns. "You showed no mercy to the two foreigners. The two foreigners did not deserve to be treated in the manner you treated them.

"A serious factor attaching to your cause is the fact that the victims trusted you to lead them to the lookout. But you betrayed the trust they had in you. You had not shown any remorse at all for what you did." Justice Lenalia said the sentence should serve as a deterrent to others who might want to engage in such activities, saying, "I will sentence you to a term much higher than the upper limit due to the very serious nature of the case."

Victoria couple attacked in Papua New Guinea

By CARLA WILSON
Times Colonist staff

A Victoria sailor is in hospital in Papua New Guinea with a fractured skull after being attacked by a man wielding a field hockey stick during a visit to an isolated tourist spot.

Leslie MacNeill, 64, could lose his left eye and may be flown to Australia for specialized care, said his partner Marcia Stromsore, 52, who was also attacked.

The James Bay couple was on an extended sailing trip on board the 11-metre Rio Nimpkish. Their plan was to head to Japan and then to Alaska and home to Victoria.

Stromsore said from Nonga Base Hospital in Port Moresby, Papua New Guinea that she is doing well, although she has a severe headache.

"I'm quite OK. I can see and I can walk," Stromsore said from the hospital Friday.

The two sailors were knocked out Tuesday at a hilltop historic site by a man who portrayed himself as a guide.

An eye specialist was to visit Mac-Neill but he may have to be flown by a chartered plane, with an accompanying doctor, to a hospital in Queensland, Australia, to see a neurosurgeon and have a CT scan. The flight cost is estimated at $20,000 and the travel would be just above sea level to ensure his medical problems are not exacerbated, Stromsore said.

Leslie MacNeill: fractured skull

They were discovered semi-conscious by a local resident and carried down from the hill on house doors serving as makeshift stretchers.

MacNeill is known in Victoria running circles as a key volunteer with the 1994 Commonwealth Games marathon and a race director of the Dallas Road Dash.

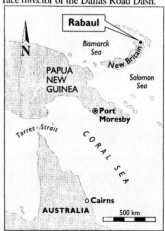

Times Colonist

Adventure turns into nightmare

Recuperation is expected to take some time. "They told me it is going to be a couple of months before we can leave here," Stromsore said.

"We'll do whatever it takes to get him better."

Dr. Arnold Waine, one of four doctors treating MacNeill, said his condition has improved. MacNeill has a fractured skull, with scalp lacerations, along with the injured eye.

When conscious, MacNeill only mumbled, Waine said. "He can listen to us, he can locate pain and he can move his arms and limbs."

"He can understand us ... That's very good."

Nicole Moen, a neighbour of Mac-Neill and Stromsore in James Bay, was horrified to hear what happened to her friends of six years. "They've been sailing for years. They come home on occasion ... It wasn't a holiday for them really. It was way of life."

The pair are lovely, low-key people, Moen said. "Very adventurous. Very fit."

"He just hit Les a couple of times and knocked him right out ... Les just fell to the ground right away."

Stromsore started screaming in case someone else was nearby. "I guess he must have hit me too because I have stitches."

The man, believed to be mentally unstable, felt he was being underpaid for painting historic items left over from the Second World War and took his anger out on them, she said.

"He didn't ask for anything. If he had asked for money, we would have given it."

The owner of the New Britain Lodge, David Loh, arranged for employees to transport the couple down the hill on house doors. "This is absolutely disgusting," Loh said.

The shocked business community of Rabaul and nearby Kokopo raised the equivalent of $900 Cdn as a reward for the capture of the man.

A 20-year-old local man has been arrested and charged with assault, said Rabaul police Det. Const. Francis Munap, however no name was released. The man is co-operating with police and expected to plead guilty, Munap said.

The Rio Nimpkish remains moored at Simpson Harbour. Stromsore said, "The people at the yacht club are just wonderful."

Beaten sailor in Australian care after assault in New Guinea

By CINDY E. HARNETT
Times Colonist staff

A James Bay sailor, whose head was pummelled in an attack in an isolated tourist spot in Papua New Guinea, has lost his eye and is now in an Australian hospital where neurosurgeons are monitoring his severe head injuries.

"In perspective, the eye is nothing," said sister Marie MacNeill, in Vancouver. "He'll put on a patch and pretend he's Capt. Bligh and he'll tell pirate stories.

"We're concerned that he regains his intellect and motor control," she said. "We don't know what the future holds but we're hopeful. He's a real fighter. He loves life and he's extremely healthy."

Michael MacNeill, 35, of Vancouver, left Saturday to be with his father who is suffering from internal bleeding, blood clots and several skull fractures. The fractures are helping relieve some of the brain swelling, said MacNeill.

The sailor is in stable condition but is mostly unconscious and confused and can't talk. He is in Townsville Hospital in Australia where there is a neurosurgical ward. Family has been assured the hospital has the latest equipment and the patient "will receive the best care he can," said his sister.

The James Bay sailor is one in a family of eight brothers and sisters living across Canada. One brother, Don MacNeill lives in Victoria.

A close family friend for more than two decades, Vickers was working the phones on the weekend trying to organize communication and set up a trust fund to help the family with expenses. The Toronto Dominion account will be finalized and publicized Monday, said Vickers.

Considering the time needed for recuperation, doctors said it may be months before MacNeill is able to return home, she reported. "He's a very close friend and very active member of the community, the running community, the boating community, the health-care community."

Vickers and MacNeill were respiratory therapists recruited to Victoria, to work at Victoria General Hospital, from Alberta.

"Since we all work in health care we know that you need prompt attention and its going to cost money. That's why we're moving fast to set up a trust fund," said Vickers, now a business consultant.

MacNeill has a daughter and stepson in Victoria as well as a son in Vancouver and three grandchildren. A marathoner, he is well known in running circles as a participant and volunteer.

"It's just so shocking. He's such a vibrant youthful person. He's never changed. He's unbelievably fit," she said.

"We're telling them to do whatever they have to and the funds will be available," said Vickers.

Battered sailor asks for family

BY CARLA WILSON
Times Colonist staff

A Victoria sailor hospitalized in Australia asked about his grandchildren when his son arrived from Vancouver, a hopeful sign for which his family is grateful.

"It's really good news," said Anne MacNeill, whose father Leslie MacNeill was flown to Townsville Hospital in northern Australia after being attacked last week in Papua New Guinea.

The 64-year-old, who suffered a fractured skull, is under close watch by doctors. He is still slipping in and out of consciousness, his daughter said Monday in Victoria.

It's expected surgery will take place later this week to remove his left eye.

Marcia Stromsmoe, 52, MacNeill's partner, is also in hospital in Australia with less severe injuries.

She was attacked too but said a few days ago from Papua New Guinea that she was OK.

The two stopped at Papua New Guinea while on an extended sailing vacation.

A man who called himself a guide took them to a hilly tourist area, where he attacked them with a field hockey stick before fleeing.

They were discovered semi-conscious by local residents and taken to hospital before being transported to Australia on the weekend. A 20-year-old man was arrested.

MacNeill's 39-year-old son, Michael, flew to Australia to be at his father's beside; Anne is also considering travelling there this week.

MacNeill said her father recognized Michael. "He talked to him and he asked how the kids (his three grandchildren) were.

"There's somebody watching out for him. With the extent of his injuries, he should have had brain damage.

Attack on pair horrifies sister

WENDY-ANNE THOMPSON
CALGARY HERALD

A Calgary woman whose sister was brutally attacked overseas says the experience has been "worse than sad."

"Sad does not even begin to describe what happened. To me, it's just incomprehensible that someone should be so angry at the world they would pick up a stick and hurt two totally innocent people," said Katherine King.

"It's absolutely horrifying."

King's sister, Marcia Stromsmoe, was vacationing in Papua New Guinea with her partner, Les MacNeill. The couple, who lived in Edmonton until 1995, are Victoria residents.

As the two ventured up a remote hill last week, they were joined on the trail by a 20-year-old man. When they reached the top, the man took out a field hockey stick and started viciously attacking MacNeill. He then went after Stromsmoe.

"My sister said he just suddenly hit Les and he had no time to even be aware. She said he didn't even have time to get his arm up," King said.

"She said she doesn't remember being hit, but obviously she was, because she has a cracked skull and two black eyes."

QUOTABLE

❝

She doesn't remember being hit, but … she has a cracked skull and two black eyes

❞

KATHERINE KING

AUSTRALIA

Beating victim has skull fracture

BY CARLA WILSON
Times Colonist staff

A medical test has revealed that a Victoria woman hit over the head while vacationing in Papua New Guinea has a hairline fracture in her skull.

Marcia Stromsmoe, 52, is in Townsville Hospital in Australia, along with partner Leslie MacNeill, 64, who is in more serious condition. He has been semi-conscious and is expected to lose his left eye.

Katherine King, of Calgary, was relieved to talk to her sister in hospital.

"She has a hairline fracture," King said.

"Her vision is blurry in one eye."

Stromsmoe had declared herself OK last week, but ongoing symptoms prompted doctors in Australia to order a CT scan, King said.

The hospital in Papua New Guinea did not have a CT scan machine.

"We are so thankful that they were taken to Australia," King said. It is believed Stromsmoe's injuries will heal on their own, she said.

"My sister said she has two black eyes and stitches all over her head … She's

'She has a hairline fracture. Her vision is blurry in one eye.'

Katherine King,
sister of Marcia Stromsmoe

looking forward to getting out of the hospital."

Stromsmoe is part of a large extended family, King said. She grew up southeast of Lethbridge, Alta., and studied law. She was an estate planner for an insurance company in Edmonton but lost her job when the firm was downsized. She moved to Victoria several years ago.

A trust fund has been set up to help pay for medical costs for MacNeill and Stromsmoe. Donations can be made to any TD Canada Trust branch to account 2595200134.

Family friend Shirley Vickers said, "Les and Marcia are facing astronomical costs. The air evac flight to Australia alone cost $21,000. We are initially hoping to raise $30,000 to cover the transport costs."

Bev Hyde, family friend and former wife of Leslie MacNeill, said insurance will not cover all the costs.

Sailor 'doing well' after losing an eye

Times Colonist staff

Surgeons in Australia have removed Leslie MacNeill's left eye , but it will be weeks before the Victoria man who was attacked in Papua New Guinea earlier this month will be able to return home.

"He's doing well," said daughter Anne MacNeill of Victoria.

"He's still really confused. But it sounds like he is going to be able to come out of, we're hoping, barring any complications."

He has blood clots in his brain, his daughter said, but he was on his feet after his surgery late this week.

It appears it may take five to eight more weeks before Leslie MacNeill could return home on a commercial flight, Anne MacNeill said.

Harriers run to aid injured friends

Members of the Harriers running team continue to help Leslie MacNeill and Marcia Stromsmoe at the upcoming Harriers Pioneer 8K run.

MacNeill and Stromsmoe, both Harriers themselves, were badly injured in a December attack in Papua New Guinea. All proceeds from the run will go to a fund set up to assist with medical and transportation expenses.

The fund, established through TD Canada Trust, has been supported at a number of running events in recent weeks.

Battle-scarred duo home after New Guinea attack

By Gerard Young
Times Colonist staff

It wasn't the way Leslie MacNeill and Marcia Stromsmoe hoped to close out their five-year sailing adventure. One moment the James Bay couple was enjoying the mid-day view around Rabaul, Papua New Guinea, the next they were being whacked by a field hockey stick.

MacNeill, 65, is in Victoria General Hospital, following the pair's arrival home Tuesday. He lost his left eye in the Dec. 11 attack and suffered head injuries.

Stromsmoe, 52, still bears the scars from stitches on her forehead and the back of her skull where she was struck.

MacNeill, a former hospital respiratory therapist, was in the neurological unit Thursday, but Stromsmoe said she expected his stay to be short though he would need some therapy.Papua New Guinea police have a 22-year-old man in custody and have charged him with attempted murder.

"It wouldn't stop me from going back," Stromsmoe said Thursday on her way to Vic General to visit her partner. "Wrong place at the wrong time."

The couple set sail five years ago this coming September on the 11.9-metre Rio Nimpkish. They had been in Australia, after more than 18 months in New Zealand and two years in Mexico.

They had planned to sail to Japan and on to to Alaska before coming home this fall, said Stromsmoe, who shares a

Marcia Stromsmoe and Leslie Mac-Neill before Papua New Guinea visit.

Toronto Street home with MacNeill.

They planned to stay over Christmas and New Year's in Papua New Guinea, an independent country boasting 867 languages in a mixed-race population of more than four million.

They decided Dec. 11 to hike up a hill to get a view of the region, which had been hit hard by a volcano eruption in 1994. Along the way, Stromsmoe said, they met a young man.

"He was a nice guy. He spoke English. There was no reason at all to be apprehensive. He was talking to us, pointing out sights along the way."

The man carried what he said was a field hockey stick, explaining he played the sport. At the top of the mountain, he suddenly smashed MacNeill with the stick, Stromsmoe said.

"It came out of the blue," she said.

He then turned on her. Someone came along and helped the pair to the hospital. The incident happened around lunchtime, but she remembers little until about suppertime when it was dark, she said.

It appears the man had no motive for the attack as they were not robbed, she said, suggesting he was mentally unstable.

But Ephraim Tomonmow, chief police superintendent for New Britain province, said in a telephone interview Thursday that it's believed the attacker had a beef with a local hotel over not being paid. He decided to target tourists so as to scare them away from the hotel, he said.

If convicted of attempted murder, the man could face up to 14 years in prison.

The suspect, a local villager with no criminal history, was arrested the day after the assault, he said.

MacNeill was well enough to fly home with Stromsmoe on a commercial flight but immediately went to VGH for followup treatment. He was put in isolation as a precaution. Stromsmoe said MacNeill is coming around and she expects him to make a full recovery.

The sailboat remains at a Papua New Guinea yacht club. She will accompany MacNeill if he goes back to retrieve it. Otherwise someone else will bring it home.

She never liked sailing but it was a chance for the two to see the world on a more affordable budget, she said. But she would go back to Papua New Guinea without fear, she said.

"I'm a bit of a fatalist. It could just as well have been getting hit by a bus crossing Douglas Street."

But a trip to the hospital in Victoria would be far less costly. The air ambulance that flew MacNeill back to an Australian hospital cost $21,000 US, said family friend Shirley Vickers.

She and other friends are fundraising to help the couple with the costs. A dance and silent auction have been organized for Jan. 19 at the Royal Victoria Yacht Club.

Marcia Stromsmoe and Les MacNeill stand aboard the recently returned Rio Nimpkish at Fisherman's Wharf.   *Darren Stone/Times Colonist*

BACK AT HOME

Sailing friends come to aid of Victoria couple after brutal attack thwarts quest to circle globe

BY JEFF BELL
Times Colonist staff

In a perfect world, Marcia Stromsmoe and Les MacNeill would be just about ready to round the southern tip of Vancouver Island, homeward-bound to Victoria after a five-year sailing adventure.

Instead, they flew home in early January after being assaulted the month before in Papua New Guinea. Their sailboat, the 12-metre Rio Nimpkish, was left behind with no immediate plans for its return.

But thanks to two of the couple's friends, David Player and Paul Lim, and Player's 16-year-old son James, the Rio Nimpkish is finally back in familiar waters. The trio flew to Papua New Guinea at the beginning of May and set sail for Victoria a short time later.

The Rio Nimpkish floated into Victoria harbour a few days ago through a cur-

tain of afternoon fog. The boat is berthed now at Fisherman's Wharf.

David Player expressed the sentiment Stromsmoe and MacNeill might have had, if fate had allowed them to make the final leg of their voyage.

"It's a fantastic feeling coming into Victoria after all those miles," he said.

Despite the nightmarish turn their dream trip took, MacNeill said there was some excitement in seeing the Rio Nimpkish again. After all, it had taken him and Stromsmoe to Mexico, New Zealand and Australia before they put into port in Papua New Guinea, where they planned to spend Christmas and New Year's before turning to northern climes.

Stromsmoe, 53, and MacNeill, 65, have begun to put the horror of the attack behind them.

Couple: 'It was a case of wrong place, wrong time'

• From Page A1

MacNeill, the more seriously hurt of the two, is back in the couple's James Bay home after a long period of medical treatment. He still needs rehabilitative therapy at Gorge Road Hospital.

He lost an eye, Stromsmoe said, and the head injuries affected his speech and his short-term memory.

"Physically, though, he's just great. He goes running three times a week for about an hour at a time."

MacNeill's outlook is an inspiration, Stromsmoe said. "Les is amazing. He refuses to let this ruin his life. He knows he's not going to be as good as he was, but he says he's going to be as good as he is able to be."

In addition to getting back to running, MacNeill said he is taking saxophone lessons to rediscover an instrument he once played.

Sailing seems unfamiliar to him, he said, as he stood on the deck of the Rio Nimpkish.

"I'll have to learn it all again now."

Stromsmoe, who ended up with stitches in her forehead and the back of her skull, has also made progress in recent months. "But I've lost my sense of smell, so food doesn't taste as good."

Stromsmoe said the Players and Lim did an incredible thing in bringing the Rio Nimpkish home for them. David Player responded that the substitute crew was happy to help, especially after seeing how well Stromsmoe and MacNeill are doing.

"That was all the reward we needed for what we did."

MacNeill said he and Stromsmoe are also grateful for all of the other support they have received from friends and from the public, including the staging of several events to assist them to deal with costs incurred after the attack.

"There has been some incredibly wonderful people," MacNeill said.

Stromsmoe said the attack is not typical of Papua New Guinea, and should not make people think badly of the country.

"It was a case of wrong place, wrong time," she said.

What is Acquired Brain Injury?

ACQUIRED BRAIN INJURY (ABI) is defined by the World Health Organization as damage to the brain that occurs after birth, and is not related to a congenital or degeneration disease. This damage may be temporary or permanent, and may cause partial or functional disability or psychosocial maladjustment. (Geneva Convention, 1996)

Possible causes include, but are not limited to, car accident, physical assault, fall, concussion, industrial accident, stroke, aneurysm, brain tumour, infection such as meningitis, toxic exposure such as to carbon dioxide or solvents, or lack of oxygen such as near drowning or diving accident.

It is estimated that 1.5%, or 2,103 persons, of Central Vancouver Island's population of 140,200 suffer from acquired brain injuries each year. ABI is the number one killer and disabler of people under the age of 45. More than 50% of people with ABI are under the age of 20. 14,000 British Columbians are newly diagnosed with an ABI each year and 160,000 live with the devastating impacts. ABI costs Canadians more than $1 billion per year.

About the Author

L ES MACNEILL WAS BORN in Halifax, Nova Scotia, in 1936, the second of eight children. After a career in retail sales and investment fund management, which took him from St. John's to Victoria, he worked in respiratory therapy at Victoria General Hospital for over 20 years.

An avid runner, Les often wins his age category in road races, and has completed a triathlon. As an active running club member, he has acted as a race director and as volunteer co-ordinator for the Commonwealth Games.

A lifelong sailor, Les circumnavigated Vancouver Island and sailed single-handed to Alaska. After taking early retirement in 1995, with his partner Marcia Stromsmoe, he sailed to Mexico, French Polynesia, Niue, the Cook Islands, Tonga, New Zealand and Australia. In 2001, while en route home, they were brutally attacked in Papua New Guinea. Les suffered 8 skull fractures and extensive brain injury, and spent many months in therapy.

He and Marcia now live in Victoria where he continues to run and make music. He has three children and four grandchildren.

ISBN 142513153-0

9 781425 131531